The Unofficial Starbucks Cookbook
in Less than 5 Minutes:

Your Go-To Starbucks Book For Preparing Your Favorite Drinks At
Home and Saving Money

Aubrianne Cooke

Discover 12 BONUS Starbucks Copycat Recipes You Can Make from Home in Less Than 5 Minutes!

As a way of saying "thank you" for your purchase, I'm going to share with you a free Gift that is exclusive to readers of The Unofficial Starbucks Cookbook in Less Than 5 Minutes

It will teach you how to prepare 12 of your favorite recipes in no time and save major cash!

Table of Contents

Introduction

Ever fall in love with a limited-edition flavor at Starbucks only to have it be out of season or already sold out for the day? Never again with this beverage bible! Now you will be able to enjoy your favorite recipes all year round or whenever the mood strikes you. Enjoy a Smore's Frappuccino in January or a Peppermint Mocha in March. Never again miss the deadline for a Pumpkin Spice Latte. You are the captain of your own flavor ship.

Starbucks has become a go-to for fun, festive, and delicious drinks. Frozen, Blended, Steamed, Swirled, Steeped, Whipped, or Frothy there truly is a drink for everyone. With this book, you will be able to create tasty beverages right at home in under 5 minutes.

While all recipes are measured and tested to be as close to drinking to the real thing, feel free to tweak them to best suit your palate. For sugars try these alternative sweeteners: monk fruit extract, agave nectar, stevia extract or powder, honey, maple syrup, or allulose. For milk alternatives: coconut, soy, oat, and almond milk are great options. Coconut Cream can also be a great alternative to Heavy Whipping Cream in some instances.

Each recipe is measured to be one large serving size of beverage unless otherwise noted. There are many sauces and syrups that you can buy ready-made if you choose to skip the fully from scratch part of the recipe. The prep time on all recipes is 5 minutes or less unless noted at the top of the instructions with an *asterisk.

Most recipes in this book will require a few simple kitchen equipment items:

- Small pot or kettle

- Blender

- Whisk or mixer with a whisk attachment

- Saucepan

- Large spoon

- Sieve or strainer

- Mugs or serving glasses, straws, lids, etc.

We encourage you to make every beverage your own. Be your own Barista and save loads of cash at the same time. **Enjoy!**

Refreshers
Refreshing Cold Drinks

Strawberry Acai Refresher

Ingredients:

2 cups Sugar
1 Tbsp Acai Powder
3 cups Water, cold
1/2 cup sliced Strawberries, freeze-dried or fresh
1/2 Apple Juice
1 cup Ice

Instructions:

To make the syrup base:

1. Pour 2 cups of water with all the sugar into a pot and bring to a boil.

2. When the sugar has dissolved, about 3 minutes.

3. Turn the sugar water temperature down to a simmer and whisk the Acai Powder and half of the strawberries in.

To Assemble the Beverage:

4. Strain the berries from the syrup and add the apple juice. Then let it cool.

   ‣ This syrup can be kept refrigerated for up to 2 weeks and used as needed.

5. Mix1 cup water with ice and pour 1/3 cup prepared syrup over the ice water and garnish with sliced strawberries, either fresh or freeze-dried.

   ‣ You can adjust the sweetness by adding less or more syrup to your cup.

Mango Dragonfruit Refresher

Ingredients:

1 cup Sugar
1 cup Water
1 cup Mango pieces
1/2 cup Dragonfruit pieces or Juice
1 tsp Green Coffee Powder or Extract
1 cup Ice

Instructions:

1. If using frozen fruit or purees allow them to defrost a little.

2. Bring the water and sugar to a boil until the sugar dissolves then let it cool off the heat.

3. In a blender add the mango and dragonfruit, pour the warm (not hot) sugar water over the fruit and add the Green Coffee Powder.

4. Blend until smooth.

5. Strain the mixture over ice and enjoy!

   ‣ You can adjust the sweetness by adding less or more water to your cup.

   ‣ The strained mixture will keep refrigerated for up to 1 week, always shake or stir before using after it has sat chilled to distribute any flavor particles that have settled at the bottom.

Very Berry Hibiscus Refresher

Ingredients:

1 cup Water
1 Tbsp Dried Hibiscus Flowers or Jamaica
3 Tbsp Agave Nectar
1/2 cup Raspberries, defrost if frozen
1/2 cup Strawberries, defrost of frozen
1 cup Ice
1 cup Club Soda or unflavored Sparkling Water
Lime Slices

*Prep time total: 16 minutes

Instructions:

For the Hibiscus Tea:

1. Place the dried flowers in a small pan and cover with water

2. Once the water has boiled lower the heat to a simmer for 5 minutes.

3. Turn off the heat and add the agave to the water. Let the tea mixture steep for 10 minutes.

4. Strain the flowers from the water and set aside.

To Assemble the Beverage:

5. Place the berries in a pitcher or divided into individual glasses and smash them with a large spoon.

6. Place Ice over the berries and add lime slices.

7. Fill the pitcher or glasses 3/4 way up with the sweetened Hibiscus tea.

8. Top with Soda Water and drink your cares away.

    ‣ You can adjust the sweetness by adding less or more soda water or agave to the drink.

    ‣ The tea will keep refrigerated for up to 2 weeks, always shake or stir before using after it has sat chilled.

Pink Drink

Begin with the Strawberry Acai Refresher Recipe

Then add:

1 cup Unsweetened Lowfat Coconut Milk

Instructions:

1. Mix together 1 cup of water, the coconut milk, ice, and pour 1/3 cup prepared syrup in.

2. Garnish with sliced strawberries, either fresh or freeze-dried.

   ‣ You can adjust the sweetness by adding less or more syrup to your cup.

   ‣ Stevia makes a great alternative to sugar syrup in this recipe.

   ‣ Half-and-Half Milk can be subbed for the coconut milk for a richer drink.

Dragonfruit Lemonade Refresher

Begin with the Mango Dragonfruit Refresher Recipe

Then add:

2 cups Lemonade or mixed Lemonade Powder mixed in 2 cups of Water

Instructions:

1. Strain the fruit from the liquid and mix it with the prepared lemonade.

2. Pour the bright pink juice over ice and enjoy!

   ‣ You can adjust the sweetness by adding less or more water to your cup.

Blended Strawberry Lemonade

Ingredients:

1/2 cup Sugar
1 Tbsp Acai Powder
1 cup Water
1/2 cup sliced Strawberries, fresh or frozen
2 cups Ice
3 cups Lemonade or mixed Lemonade Powder mixed-in 2 cups of Water

Instructions:

To make the syrup base:
1.   boil the water with all the sugar.

2.   Turn the sugar water temperature down to a simmer and whisk the Acai Powder and half of the strawberries in.

3.   Simmer for 3 minutes or until the sugar is fully dissolved. Then remove from the heat.

4.   Strain the berries from the syrup and let it cool.

   ‣ This syrup can be kept refrigerated for up to 2 weeks and used as needed.

To Assemble the Beverage:

5.   Mix the prepared lemonade with the syrup in a blender cup and add ice to fill.

6.   Blend the mixture until thick and smooth.

7.   Pour into glasses and enjoy.

   ‣ You can adjust the sweetness by adding less or more syrup to your cup.

   ‣ You may find that the syrup is not needed depending on the sweetness of your lemonade mixture.

Pineapple Matcha

Ingredients:

1 cup Water
1 cup Sugar
1 bag Ginger Tea
1/2 cup Pineapple Juice
1 cup Coconut Milk
1 tsp Matcha Green Tea Powder
1 cup Ice

*Prep time total: 9 minutes

Instructions:

1. Place the water and sugar in a pan over medium heat and bring to a boil for 3 minutes or until the sugar is dissolved.

2. Place the teabag into the sugar water and let it steep for 5 minutes.

3. In a large pitcher pour the pineapple juice and the green tea powder and whisk well.

4. Pour the coconut milk into the pitcher and whisk until combined.

5. Add the ice and stir.

6. Remove the teabag from the simple syrup and pour over the iced mixture.

   ‣ You can adjust the sweetness by adding more or less simple syrup or plain water.

   ‣ If you like your drink with more of a zippy tang, add less sugar and more pineapple juice.

   ‣ If your green tea powder tends to lump and not dissolve well by whisking, try to make this mixture in a blender before pouring it over ice.

Violet Drink

Ingredients:

2 cups Water
1 cup Sugar
1/2 cup Blueberries
1/2 cup Blackberries (reserve a few for garnish)
1 bag Passion Fruit Herbal or Green Tea
1 cup Soy or Coconut Milk
1 cup Ice

* Prep time total: 7 minutes

Instructions:

1. Steep the tea in 1 cup of hot water for 6 minutes.

2. Place the berries and sugar in a pan and cover with 1 cup of water.

3. Simmer the berries on low heat while stirring often until they burst a bit and the sugar granules disappear.

4. Let the berry juice mixture cool.

5. Remove the teabag from the water and add the tea water to the berry juice pan.

6. Strain the berries from the juice.

   ‣ This juice base can be kept refrigerated for up to 1 week as is.

7. Place ice in your desired glass and pour the milk 1/2 way up, then add the berry juice to fill up the cup.

8. Garnish with blackberries and sip, sip, sip.

   ‣ Fresh or frozen berries work for the drink base.

Passion Tea Lemonade

Ingredients:

2 cups Water
1 Tbsp Sugar
1/4 tsp Vanilla Extract
1 cup Lemonade
1 bag Passion Fruit Tea
Lemon Slices for garnish
2 cups Ice

* Prep time total: 7 minutes

Instructions:

1. In a pot over medium heat bring the water and sugar to a boil.

2. Lower the heat and add the vanilla and teabag and simmer for 2 minutes.

3. Turn the heat off the pan and let the mixture sit for 4 minutes.

4. Remove the teabag from the pan and discard, let the tea water continue to cool.

5. In a tall glass pour the lemonade over ice 3/4 way up.

6. Pour the tea mixture over to fill to the top.

7. Give it a gentle stir and garnish with lemon slices.

› Tazo brand tea is preferred for the best color and flavor.

› The vanilla tricks your brain that there is more sugar in this drink than there is, but if you find the drink not sweet enough adding agave nectar or stevia are great additions that will dissolve well added last minute.

Black Tea Lemonade

Ingredients:

2 cups Water
1 Tbsp Sugar
1 cup Mango Juice
1 cup Lemonade
1 bag Black Tea
Lemon Slices for garnish
2 cups Ice

*Prep time total: 7 minutes

Instructions:

1. In a pot over medium heat bring the water and sugar to a boil for 2 minutes.

2. Turn off the heat for the pot and add the teabag. Let the mixture sit for 4 minutes to steep deeply.

3. Remove the teabag from the pot and discard, let the tea continue to cool.

4. Stir together the mango juice and lemonade.

5. In a pitcher or individual glasses pour the mango lemonade over ice 3/4 way up.

6. Pour over the tea mixture to fill to the top.

7. Give it a gentle stir and garnish with lemon slices.

   ‣ Earl Grey or English Breakfast are great teas to use for this caffein-ated beverage.

   ‣ If mango juice is difficult to acquire, you could use frozen fruit and puree it with water until thin but not watery. Just make sure to strain any fruit chunks first if planning to sip through a straw.

Lattes
Milky drinks, cold and hot

Vanilla Iced Chai Latte

Ingredients:

1 cup Water
1/2 cup sugar
1 Tbsp Vanilla Extract
1 bag Chai Tea
1 cup Milk, 2% or milk alternative
1 cup Ice
Whipped Cream and Caramel Sauce for Topping

* Prep time total: 12 minutes

Instructions:

1. In a pot, heat the water and the sugar until the sugar is dissolved.

2. Remove the simple syrup from the heat and add the vanilla and teabag.

3. Cover and let the tea steep for at least 10 minutes.

4. In a glass full of ice pour 1/3 cup tea mixture to every 1 cup of cold milk.

5. Stir gently and top with whipped cream and maybe a little drizzle of caramel sauce.

Pumpkin Spice Latte

Ingredients:

1/3 cup Brown Sugar
1 Tbsp Pumpkin Puree
1 tsp Pumpkin Pie Spice
1 tsp Vanilla Extract
1 shot Espresso or Black Coffee
1 cup Milk, 2% or milk alternative
Whipped Cream and Ground Cinnamon for topping

Instructions:

1. In a blender add the brown sugar, pumpkin puree, pumpkin spice, vanilla, and hot espresso and whip until well mixed.

2. Warm the milk, do not boil, whisking to froth if desired.

3. In a mug or glass add the pumpkin mixture from the blender and pour the steamed milk on top, stir gently.

4. Top with whipped cream and a sprinkle of cinnamon and enjoy!

Iced Caramel Latte

Ingredients:

1/3 cup Milk
1/2 cup Cold Brewed Coffee
1 Tbsp Caramel Sauce
1 cup Ice

Instructions:

1. Add the ice to a tall glass.

2. Pour the cold coffee brewed over the ice, followed by the milk.

3. Stir in the caramel sauce.

    ‣ This recipe relies on the caramel to sweeten the drink and can be lessened or increased to your taste.

    ‣ Good quality or dark roast coffee will result in better coffee flavor.

    ‣ You can of course top with cream and more caramel as desired.

Cinnamon Dolce Latte

Ingredients:

2 cups Brown Sugar
1 Tbsp Ground Cinnamon
2 cups Water
1 cup Milk, 2% or milk alternative
1 cup Coffee, brewed
Whipped Cream

* Prep time total: 10 minutes

Instructions:

To make the Cinnamon Syrup:

1. In a heavy pot bring to boil the water, sugar, and cinnamon.

2. Reduce heat and stir occasionally until the sugar is all dissolved. About 8 minutes.

3. Let the cinnamon syrup cool.

Continue making the beverage:

4. Warm the milk gently, do not boil.

5. Add in a mug or glass pour 1 cup of coffee, 1 cup milk, and 1/3 cup of the cinnamon syrup.

6. Top with a little whipped cream.

Peppermint Mocha Latte

Ingredients:

1 cup water
1/4 cup Sugar
1/4 cup Cocoa Powder
1/2 cup Coffee, brewed
1 tsp peppermint extract
1 cup Milk, 2% or milk alternative
Candy Cane Crumbs and Whipped Cream for topping

Instructions:

To make the Chocolate Sauce:

1. Bring to boil the water, sugar, and cocoa whisking slowly for 5 minutes.

2. Remove from the heat.

   ‣ This mixture can be cooled and store refrigerated for up to 2 weeks for later use.

Continue making the beverage:

3. Steam the milk, do not boil, gently warm.

4. Stir the peppermint extract into the milk.

5. In a mug pour 1 cup of warm pepperminty milk, 1 cup coffee, and 1/3 cup chocolate sauce.

6. Stir and top with whipped cream and a sprinkle of candy cane.

   ‣ Using a strong dark roast coffee or even espresso to help the coffee flavor not hide behind all the chocolate and peppermint.

Caramel Brûlée Latte

Ingredients:

1/2 cup Water
1/3 cup Brown Sugar
1 tsp Butter
1 tsp Vanilla Extract
1/2 cup Milk
1 cup Black Coffee, brewed
Whipped Cream and Turbinado or Raw Sugar for topping

* Prep time total: 7 minutes

Instructions:

1. Boil the water and sugar until the sugar is dissolved, about 4 minutes.

2. Reduce the heat and add the butter to simmer for another 2 minutes.

3. Remove the pan from the heat and add the milk and vanilla.

4. In a mug add the brewed coffee then the sweet milk mixture to taste.

5. Top with whipped cream and raw sugar if desired.

    ‣ The brown sugar helps to give the drink that carmel-esque flavor of a creme brûlée.

Iced Matcha Latte

Ingredients:

1/2 cup water
1/2 cup Sugar
2 tsp Matcha Green Tea Powder
1 cup Milk, 2% or milk alternative
1 cup Ice

Instructions:

To make a Simple Syrup:

1. Boil the sugar and water to make a simple syrup.

2. When the sugar is dissolved, lower the heat for 2 minutes, then let cool.

Continue with the beverage:

3. In a glass add the Matcha powder with the milk and stir well.

4. Add Ice to the green milk.

5. Pour the simple syrup into the glass and stir, tasting as you go to get the right sweetness.

    ‣ Typically 2 tablespoons of simple syrup is plenty to sweeten 1 cup of milk.

Iced Mocha Latte

Ingredients:

1/3 cup Sugar
1/3 cup Cocoa Powder
1/3 cup Water
1 tsp Vanilla Extract
1 cup Coffee, brewed
1/2 cup Milk, 2% or milk alternative
1 cup Ice
Whipped Cream for topping

Instructions:

For Chocolate Sauce:

1. Whisk together in a pot the sugar, cocoa, and water and bring to a simmer for 3 minutes while stirring slowly.

2. Pull the chocolate sauce off the heat and stir in the vanilla. Set aside.

Continue with the beverage:

3. In a cup add the coffee over ice, then add the milk.

4. Swirl in 2 tablespoons of chocolate sauce and mix well.

5. Top with whipped cream and a little chocolate sauce and serve.

   ‣ Any leftover chocolate sauce can be kept chilled for up to 2 weeks.

Eggnog Latte

Ingredients:

1 cup Milk, 2% or milk alternative
2 cups Eggnog
1 shot Espresso or 1 cup of Coffee
Ground Nutmeg

Instructions:

1. Steam the milk by slowly heating it in a pan and whisking lightly.

2. Pull the milk off the heat and stir the eggnog into the milk.

3. In a mug or glass add the espresso or coffee and top with warm eggnog mix.

4. Sprinkle the top with ground nutmeg and serve immediately.

   ‣ Once eggnog has been heated it will not keep very long without spoiling.

   ‣ You can whisk or even place the milk in a blender to make it frothier.

London Fog Latte

Ingredients:

1 bag Earl Grey Black Tea
1/2 tsp dried Lavender
1/2 tsp Vanilla Extract
1 Tbsp Honey
1/2 cup water
1/2 cup Milk, 2% or milk alternative

* Prep time total: 8 minutes

Instructions:

1. Boil the water and pour over the tea, lavender, and vanilla and let steep for 6 minutes.

2. Heat the milk, do not boil, gently warm.

3. In a mug or glass add the warm milk and stir in the honey until well mixed.

4. Strain the teabag and lavender petals from the water.

5. Add the steeped water into the mug and swish gently to mix.

6. Enjoy your London Fog.

   ‣ Using Lavender Honey would be a nice touch.

   ‣ For a non-caffeinated version use an herbal tea with lavender and other herbs and omit the extra dried lavender.

Frappes
Blended Beverages

S'mores Frappe

Ingredients:

1 shot Espresso
1 Tbsp Sugar
1 Tbsp Cocoa Powder
2 Tbsp Honey
1 cup Milk, 2% or milk alternative
2 cups Ice
1 Tbsp Marshmallow Whip Topping
1 large Graham Cracker
More Marshmallow and Graham for Topping

Instructions:

To make a Mocha Sauce:

1. In a small pot whisk the sugar, cocoa, and honey with the espresso until the granules of sugar have dissolved and there are no cocoa lumps to make a mocha sauce.

Continue with the beverage:

2. In the cup of a blender add the milk and ice.

3. In the glass or cup you will serve the Frappe in, drizzle a little of the mocha sauce into the cup to just coat the inside.

4. Pour the rest of the mocha sauce into the blender.

5. Add the graham and marshmallow whip to the blender and whip until the ice is broken down.

6. Pour the smooth Frappe into the prepared cup and top with more Marshmallow and Graham.

Double Chocolate Chip Frappe

Ingredients:

1/2 cup Water
1/4 cup Sugar
2 Tbsp Cocoa Powder
1/4 tsp Vanilla Extract
1 cup Milk, whole, skim, or milk alternative
2 cups Ice
1/4 cup Mini Chocolate Chips
Whipped Cream and more chocolate chips for topping

Instructions:

To make a Chocolate Sauce:

1. In a small pot whisk the water, sugar, cocoa until the granules of sugar have dissolved and there are no cocoa lumps to make a chocolate sauce.

2. Let the sauce cool and stir in the vanilla.

Continue with the Frappe:

3. In the cup of a blender add the milk, chocolate chips, and ice.

4. In the glass or cup you will serve the Frappe in, drizzle a little of the sauce into the cup to just coat the inside.

5. Pour the rest of the sauce into the blender.

6. Whip in the blender until the ice is broken down and a smooth texture,

7. Pour the Frappe into your prepared glass and top with whipped cream and more mini chocolate chips.

   ‣ Using a fattier milk will make the drink richer.

Strawberries & Creme Frappe

Ingredients:

1/4 cup Strawberries, fresh or frozen
2 Tbsp Honey
1/4 cup Water
3/4 cup Milk of choice
1/2 cup Vanilla Ice Cream
1 cup Ice
Strawberry slices and Whipped Cream for topping

Instructions:

1. In a small pot simmer the strawberries, honey, and water for 4 minutes on low heat or until the berries start to mush.

2. In the cup of a blender add the milk and strawberry mixture from the pot and blend until very smooth and pink.

3. Next, add the ice cream and ice to the blender and whip until smooth and creamy.

4. Pour the Frappe into a tall glass and top with whipped cream and some sliced strawberries.

Birthday Cake Frappe

Ingredients:

1/2 cup Heavy Whipping Cream
2 Tbsp Powdered Sugar
1/8 tsp or a drop of red or pink food dye
1 cup Milk of choice
1 cups Ice
1/2 cup Vanilla Ice Cream
1/4 cup Hazelnut Flavored Creamer
Colorful Sprinkles for topping

Instructions:

To make Pink Whipped Cream Topping:

1. In a bowl used for whipping add the heavy cream, powdered sugar, and food dye and whip until fluffy.

2. Add the pink whipped cream to a piping bag, preferably with a star tip for a neat look.

Continue making the beverage:

3. In the cup of a blender add the milk, ice, ice cream, and creamer and whip until very smooth.

4. Pour the Frappe into a glass or cup and pipe the top with the pink whipped cream and a dash of sprinkles to serve.

   ‣ As an alternative to Hazelnut Creamer, you can mix 1/4 tsp hazelnut or almond-flavored extract and 1/4 cup milk.

Mocha Frappe

Ingredients:

1/4 cup Water
3 Tbsp Sugar
3 Tbsp Cocoa Powder
2 Tbsp Honey
1 shot Espresso
1/2 cup Milk, 2% or milk alternative
1 cup Ice
Whipped Cream for topping

Instructions:

To make a Chocolate Sauce:

1. In a small pot whisk the water, sugar, cocoa, and honey until the granules of sugar have dissolved and there are no cocoa lumps to make a chocolate sauce.

Continue making the beverage:

2. In the cup of a blender add the espresso, milk, and ice.

3. In the glass or cup you will serve the Frappe in, drizzle a little of the sauce into the cup to just coat the inside.

4. Pour 1/3 cup of the sauce into the blender and pulse until smooth in texture.

5. Pour the Frappe into the prepared glass and top with whipped cream and any leftover chocolate sauce.

Cotton Candy Frappe

Ingredients:

1 Tbsp Sugar
2 Tbsp seedless Raspberry Preserves or Jelly
2 Tbsp Water
1/2 tsp Vanilla Extract
2/3 cup Milk of choice
1 cup Ice
1 cup Vanilla Ice Cream
2/3 cup Vanilla Flavored Creamer
Whipped Cream for topping

Instructions:

To make the Raspberry Sauce:

1. In a small pot on low heat whisk the sugar, raspberry jam, and water until smooth and not grainy.

2. Stir in the vanilla extract into the raspberry sauce and let it cool off the heat.

Continue making the beverage:

3. In the blender cup, add the milk, ice, ice cream, creamer, and all the raspberry sauce. Blend until smooth and creamy and pink in color.

4. Pour the Frappe into a tall glass and top with fluffy whipped cream.

Chestnut Praline Frappe

Ingredients:

2 tsp Butter
5 Chestnuts, fresh or vacuum-sealed but not dried
1/3 cup Pecans
1/3 cup Sugar
1/3 cup Brown Sugar
1 cup Skim Milk or low-fat milk alternative
1 shot Espresso
2 cups Ice
Whipped Cream for topping

* Prep time total: 6 minutes

Instructions:

To make Praline Base:

1. In a small pot heated on medium-low, melt the butter, both sugars, chestnuts, and pecans stirring constantly for 2 minutes or until the nuts are a little toasted and the sugars start to melt.

   ‣ Be sure to not burn the sugars.

2. Remove a few pecan pieces to a heat-safe plate or bowl to use for topping.

Continue with the beverage:

3. Add the milk to the pot and stir occasionally. Do not boil the milk, lightly heat for about 3 minutes.

4. In a blender add the espresso and milk-nut mixture and buzz until a smooth mixture forms.

5. Add the Ice and buzz until cold and smooth.

6. Chop the reserved pecans.

7. Pour the Frappe into a tall glass and top with whipped cream and some chopped sweet pecans.

Salted Caramel Mocha Frappe

Ingredients:

2 Tbsp Sugar
2 Tbsp Cocoa Powder
1 shot Espresso
1 cup Milk of choice
3/4 cup Hazelnut Flavored Creamer
2 Tbsp Caramel Sauce, plus more for garnishment
1/2 tsp Sea Salt
2 cups Ice
Whipped Cream and more Caramel Sauce for topping

Instructions:

To make a Mocha Sauce:

1. In a small pot on low heat whisk the sugar and cocoa with the espresso until the granules of sugar have dissolved and there are no cocoa lumps. Let it cool.

Continue making the beverage:

2. In the cup of a blender add the milk, nut flavored creamer, caramel sauce, salt, and ice.

3. In the glass or cup you will serve the Frappe in, drizzle a little of the caramel sauce into the cup to just coat the inside.

4. Puree the mocha sauce with the other ingredients already in the blender until smooth and creamy.

5. Pour the Frappe into the prepared glass and top with whipped cream and a drizzle of more caramel sauce.

   ‣ If using a less pungent type of salt such as a kosher, more may be needed to add that salty punch.

32

Java Chip Frappe

Ingredients:

1/2 cup Water
1/4 cup Sugar
2 Tbsp Cocoa Powder
1/4 tsp Vanilla Extract
1 shot Espresso
1/2 cup Milk, whole, skim, or milk alternative
2 cups Ice
1/4 cup Mini Chocolate Chips
Whipped Cream and more chocolate chips for topping

Instructions:

To make the Chocolate Sauce:

1. In a small pot whisk the water, sugar, and cocoa until the granules of sugar have dissolved and there are no cocoa lumps to make a chocolate-y sauce.

2. Let the sauce cool and stir in the vanilla.

Continue making the beverage:

3. In the cup of a blender add the espresso, milk, chocolate chips, and ice.

4. In the glass or cup you will serve the Frappe in, drizzle a little of the sauce into the cup to just coat the inside.

5. Pour the rest of the sauce into the blender.

6. Whip in the blender until the ice is broken down and a smooth texture.

7. Pour the Frappe into your prepared glass and top with whipped cream and more mini chocolate chips

   ‣ 2/3 cup Dark Roast brewed coffee can be used in place of the espresso.

Matcha Green Tea Creme Frappe

Ingredients:

2 Tbsp Matcha Green Tea Powder
1/4 cup Vanilla Flavored Creamer
1 Tbsp Sweetened Condensed Milk
1 cup Milk, whole, skim, or milk alternative
1 cup Ice
Whipped Cream and more Sweetened Condensed Milk-
for topping

Instructions:

1. In the cup of a blender add the matcha powder, creamer, condensed milk, and milk. Pulse to combine.

   ‣ Make sure these items are well blended before adding the ice. No sweetened condensed milk stuck at the bottom of the blender, and no clumps of matcha powder.

2. Add the ice and puree until smooth and creamy.

3. Pour into serving glass and top with whipped cream and more sweetened condensed milk.

Coffees
Coffee Drinks

Caffe' Americano

Ingredients:

Approximately 15 grams of espresso beans
1/2 cup Hot Water

Instructions:

1. Make a double shot espresso in a machine or by using a portafilter, or french press.

2. If using loose beans, measure and grind them very fine.

3. Your water should be approximately 170 degrees Fahrenheit.

4. Pour the water over the pressed ground beans.

5. The water should be 1 part espresso to 2 parts water.

6. Serve hot and black.

   ‣ Of course you can add cream, sugar, or milk to your liking but a true Americano is strong and hot.

Cold Brew

Ingredients:

1/4 cup ground Coffee Beans
1 cup Cold Water
1 Coffee Filter or 16 inches of Cheese Cloth
1 cup Ice

* Prep time total: 2 minutes Day ahead
* Day of prep: 1 minute

Instructions:

1. Place the coffee grounds into a lidded container with the cold water.

2. Seal tight and shake.

3. Leave the sealed container at room temperature for 10 hours.

4. Place a coffee filter or triple-layered cheesecloth over a strainer that is over a larger than the strainer bowl or serving glass.

5. Pour the cold brew over the covered strainer to remove the coffee grounds.

6. Add ice to the strained cold brew and serve.

   ‣ Sweeteners and milk can be added after the straining process when adding or pouring over ice.

   ‣ Larger batches of cold brew can be made and kept refrigerated for up to 5 days.

Caramel Macchiato

Ingredients:

1 Tbsp Salted Butter
1/4 cup Brown Sugar
1/4 tsp Vanilla Extract
2 Tbsp Heavy Cream
1 cup Dark Roast Coffee, brewed
2 Tbsp Heavy Cream
Whipped Cream for topping

Instructions:

To make Caramel Sauce:

1. In a small saucepan over medium heat the butter and sugar while whisking slowly for 1 minute.

2. Stir in the heavy cream and continue to cook for 3 minutes.

3. Remove the caramel sauce from the heat and add the vanilla extract and let cool.

Continue with the beverage:

4. In a mug stir the hot brewed coffee with heavy cream and 1 heaping tablespoon of caramel sauce.

5. Top with whipped cream and a drizzle of more caramel sauce and enjoy!

Coconut Milk Thai Coffee

Ingredients:

2 cups Dark Roast Coffee, brewed
2 cups Ice
1 cup Coconut Milk, full fat
2 Tbsp Honey
Pinch of Ground Cardamom
1/4 tsp Rose Water

Instructions:

1. Brew the coffee.

2. In a small pot on low heat warm the coconut milk with the honey.

3. Lightly whisk in the cardamom and rose water.

4. Pour the coffee and spiced coconut milk into a mug and serve immediately.

   ‣ This recipe can easily be served over ice by letting the coffee and milk cool before pouring over ice.

   ‣ Sweetened condensed milk or maple syrup can be used in place of the honey.

Vanilla Sweet Cream Cold Brew

Ingredients:

1 cup ground Coffee Beans
3 cups Cold Water
1/3 cup Half-and-Half
1 Tbsp Sweetened Condensed Milk
1/2 tsp Vanilla Extract
2 cups Ice
1 Coffee Filter or 16 inches of Cheese Cloth

* Prep time total: 2 minutes Day Ahead
* Day of prep: 1 minute

Instructions:

1. Place the coffee grounds into a lidded container with the cold water.

2. Seal tight and shake.

3. Leave the sealed container at room temperature for 10 hours.

4. Place a coffee filter or triple-layered cheesecloth over a strainer that is over a larger than the strainer bowl.

5. Pour the cold brew over the covered strainer to remove the coffee grounds.

6. Whisk together the sweetened condensed milk, vanilla, and half-and-half until well combined.

7. In a serving glass filled with ice pour about 1 cup of filtered coffee in and add the sweetened half-and-half on top watching it swirl in.

8. Serve and enjoy.

Cinnamon Almond Milk Macchiato

Ingredients:

1 1/4 cup Almond Milk
1/4 cup Vanilla Flavored Creamer
1/4 tsp Ground Cinnamon
1 cup Dark Roast Coffee, brewed
Whipped Cream and more ground cinnamon for
topping

Instructions:

1. In a small saucepan over medium, heat the almond
   milk and whisk in the cinnamon until warm.

2. In a mug add the hot brewed coffee and pour over the almond
   milk, followed by the creamer.

3. Top with whipped cream and a dash of cinnamon and enjoy.

   ‣ Placing the almond milk in a blender or using a hand blender can
     help make a little froth, although almond milk will not froth as well
     as a fattier cow's milk.

   ‣ If you like your macchiato sweeter, stevia, agave, or sweetened
     condensed milk added at the warm almond milk stage would work
     best for incorporating.

Pumpkin Cream Cold Brew

Ingredients:

1 cup ground Coffee Beans
3 cups Cold Water
1/3 cup Half-and-Half
1 Tbsp Sweetened Condensed Milk
1 Tbsp Pumpkin Puree
1/2 tsp Vanilla Extract
1/2 tsp Pumpkin Pie Spice
2 cups Ice
1 Coffee Filter or 16 inches of cheese cloth
Whipped Cream and pumpkin pie spice for topping

* Prep time total: 2 minutes Day ahead
* Day of prep: 2 minutes

Instructions:

1. Place the coffee grounds into a lidded container with the cold water.

2. Seal tight and shake.

3. Leave the sealed container at room temperature for 10 hours.

4. Place a coffee filter or triple-layered cheesecloth over a strainer set in a bowl to drain.

5. Pour the cold brew over the covered strainer to remove the coffee grounds.

6. Whisk together the sweetened condensed milk with the vanilla, half-and-half, pumpkin puree, and pumpkin spice until well combined.

7. In a serving glass filled with ice pour about 1 cup of filtered coffee in and add the sweetened pumpkin mixture. Swirl. Dollop with whipped cream and a dash of pumpkin pie spice.

Iced Cocoa Cloud Macchiato

Ingredients:

2 Egg Whites
2 Tbsp Sugar, granulated white
1/2 tsp Cream of Tartar
1/2 tsp Ground Cinnamon
1 Tbsp Cocoa Powder
1/3 cup Milk or full-fat alternative milk
1 cup Dark Roast Coffee, brewed
More Cocoa Powder for topping

Instructions:

1. Brew the coffee and let it cool.

2. Whip the egg whites, sugar, cream of tartar, cocoa, and cinnamon until it forms stiff peaks of meringue.

3. Fold the milk and egg white meringue together gently.

4. In a mug with ice top with lots of fluffy milk and egg foam 3/4 way full.

5. Slowly pour the coffee into the mug down one side while tilting the mug until full.

6. Sprinkle with a dash of cocoa and enjoy your extremely frothy beverage.

   ‣ If you like your macchiato sweeter, stevia, agave, or sweetened condensed milk added to the milk before folding with the egg would work best for incorporating.

Congrats! Note from the Author:

You've reached the end of the book!

Thank you for finishing The Unofficial Starbucks Cookbook In Less Than 5 Minutes!

Looks like you enjoyed it!

If so, would you mind taking 30 seconds to leave a quick review on Amazon?

We worked hard to bring you books that you enjoy!

Plus, it helps authors like us produce more books like this in the future!

Here's where to go to leave a review now:

Made in the USA
Middletown, DE
14 October 2023